CITIES OF THE WORLD

HONG KONG

BY R. CONRAD STEIN

W9-AHG-786

CHILDREN'S PRESS®
A Division of Grolier Publishing
New York London Hong Kong Sydney
Danbury, Connecticut

CONSULTANTS

Mary Erbaugh
Associate Professor
Department of Chinese, Translation and Linguistics
City University of Hong Kong

Linda Cornwell
Learning Resource Consultant
Indiana Department of Education

Project Editor: Downing Publishing Services
Design Director: Karen Kohn & Associates, Ltd.
Photo Researcher: Jan Izzo
Pronunciations: Courtesy of Xue Ying Fung, Chinese teacher, and Tony Breed, M.A., Linguistics, University of Chicago

NOTES ON CANTONESE PRONUNCIATION

Cantonese does not have stress the way English does. Instead, it has tones on each syllable. Tones are pitch changes. In English, pitch changes are used to show the difference between a question ("oh?") and an answer ("oh."), as well as other things. The tones are very important in Cantonese. If the wrong tone is used, a completely different word has been spoken. However, to simplify, we are not including tones in this book. The best way to learn tones is to practice with a native Chinese person from Canton or Hong Kong. Most of the pronunciations in this book are exactly as they look, with the following notes: *ah* is like *a* in father; *aw* is as in draw; *oo* is as in food; *igh* and *ie* are like the *igh* in light; *ow* and *aow* are like the *ow* in cow; *oong* is like the *oo* in book followed by the *ng* as in song; *ts* is always *ts* as in gets.

Visit Children's Press on the Internet at: http://publishing.grolier.com

Library of Congress Cataloging-in-Publication Data
Stein, R. Conrad.
      Hong Kong / by R. Conrad Stein.
         p. cm. — (Cities of the world)
      Includes bibliographical references and index.
      Summary: Examines the land, people, history, economy, and cultural life of this busy international metropolis, a former British colony that was returned to China on July 1, 1997.
      ISBN 0-516-20464-5 (lib.bdg.)   0-516-26327-7 (pbk.)
      1. Hong Kong (China)—Juvenile literature.   [1. Hong Kong (China)]
I. Title.   II. Series: Cities of the world (New York, N.Y.)
DS796.H74S74   1998
951.25—dc21
                                               97-50186
                                               CIP
                                                 AC

©1998 Children's Press, a Division of Grolier Publishing Co., Inc.
All rights reserved. Published simultaneously in Canada.
Printed in the United States of America.
1 2 3 4 5 6 7 8 9 10 R 07 06 05 04 03 02 01 00 99 98

TABLE OF CONTENTS

CHANGING OF THE GUARD   *page 5*

A CITY OF MANY FACES   *page 9*

THE SAGA OF A COLONY   *page 21*

PEOPLE AND PLEASURES   *page 33*

A HONG KONG TOUR   *page 45*

FAMOUS LANDMARKS   *page 56*

FAST FACTS   *page 58*

MAP OF HONG KONG   *page 60*

GLOSSARY   *page 61*

PHOTO CREDITS   *page 62*

INDEX   *page 63*

TO FIND OUT MORE   *page 64*

ABOUT THE AUTHOR   *page 64*

A rainstorm drenched Hong Kong on the night of June 30, 1997. Yet more than half a million of the city's residents were outside. They were drawn by the excitement of a very special ceremony taking place near the city's harbor. There, a British band dressed in red uniforms played "God Save the Queen." At midnight, soldiers slowly lowered the British flag. That flag—the Union Jack—had fluttered above Hong Kong for 155 years. At ten seconds after midnight, the red and yellow flag of the People's Republic of China was raised on the same flagpole. An estimated 1 billion people around the world viewed the ceremony on television. The changing of the flags meant that the one-time British colony of Hong Kong was now officially a part of China.

The sign on this double-decker Hong Kong tram announces the 1997 celebration of the reunification of Hong Kong with China.

Below: Two young girls on an outing at a Hong Kong park

The events at the flagpole triggered wild celebrations throughout Hong Kong. Fireworks burst in the rain-swept skies. The glare of rockets was reflected in the waters of Hong Kong's magnificent harbor. Workers danced in the streets. Business owners paid $1,000 a ticket to attend special parties held in posh hotels.

Still, many Hong Kong people quietly worried about their future. China is a Communist nation. Hong Kong's prosperity is based on a capitalistic system, which encourages people to own private businesses. Would the Communists now restrict Hong Kong's free-wheeling business practices?

Worse yet, would the new government forbid the people to choose their own leaders through democratic elections? These questions troubled Hong Kong residents, but the parties went on all night.

On that stormy night, the British Empire willingly gave its prized colony to a Communist nation. No similar transfer of power had ever occurred before in history. It seemed appropriate that such a precedent-making event should take place here. Hong Kong is a unique city. There is no place like it anywhere else in the world.

About 1 billion people watched on television as Hong Kong was handed over to China on July 1, 1997. Fireworks lit up the Hong Kong skyline in celebration as the official ceremony concluded.

FACES

Certainly, the average citizens of Hong Kong do not appear consumed with worry about their new Communist masters. Instead, they go about their work at a frenzied pace. And the people continue to welcome visitors. Tourists have traveled here for generations to enjoy the food, the sights, and the wonders of this very special city.

ARRIVING

Every year, more than 6 million visitors come to Hong Kong. Most tourists arrive by air. As their plane sweeps low, passengers gaze out the windows. At first, they see barren mountains and rocky islands dotting the sea. Suddenly, a huge city emerges from this rugged landscape. The city is made up of high-rise buildings that stand like twin forests separated by Hong Kong Harbor. This strip of water, about 1 mile (1.6 kilometers) in width, is a natural harbor that makes the city one of the world's greatest seaports. North of the harbor is the Kowloon Peninsula and mainland China. South of the channel is Hong Kong Island.

Even when seen from the air, Hong Kong stirs one's imagination. It is an urban beehive, where 6.3 million people live virtually on top of one another. Every tourist knows this place contains a touch of magic. It is a Chinese city that lived under the British flag for more than 150 years. This background makes Hong Kong Asia's most international metropolis. It is a crossroads where the four corners of the world all come together.

The plane lands at Hong Kong's new Chek Lap Kok Airport. The field was built with the help of gigantic bulldozers that gouged out entire

Hong Kong Harbor and the city skyline with Victoria Peak in the background

Kowloon (KOW-LOON)
Chek Lap Kok (TSSAYK-LAHP-KAWK)
Lantau (LAHN-TAOW)

mountains and used the fill to construct two runways in the South China Sea. It was the only place where crowded Hong Kong had room to build an airport. After landing, tourists take a train to the center of town. At one point,

Tourists on a busy Hong Kong market street

passengers cross over the Lantau Link, the longest rail and auto suspension bridge in the world. The air terminal and its access way cost billions of dollars. However, Hong Kong is a city willing to gamble. Its leaders believe the new air-port will bring in more tourists and businesspeople and soon pay back the huge outlay of money.

At last, the visitor arrives in the center of Hong Kong. Lines of gleaming glass-and-steel towers create canyons. Through the canyons flow rivers of cars, trucks, dou-ble-decker buses, trams, and people on foot. City dwellers rush about as if in a race against time. The tourist struggles to define the busy street scenes.

Subway tickets are sold from machines like this one.

成人車費 Adult Fares

九龍
Kowloon

港島
Hong Kong Island

機號 C2

Nikon

Tamron

BRIEF IMPRESSIONS

What is it like to see Hong Kong for the first time? If a person confined his or her feelings to one-word impressions, such a list might read like this: crowded, modern, noisy, busy.

Crowded. In Hong Kong, pedestrians wait in crowds to cross the street with the green light. A tourist joins the pushing and shoving crowds and discovers it takes three light changes just to reach the intersection. Some Kowloon neighborhoods hold more than a quarter of a million people per 1 square mile (2.6 km^2). Those neighborhoods are the tightest-packed city blocks on earth. Indoors and outdoors, the average Hong Kong resident cannot turn around without bumping into another person. A working-class family of five lives in a flat about the size of an American one-car garage. In the poorest homes, several families share a single kitchen and a doorless toilet.

In Hong Kong, pedestrians are jammed together on crowded streets and busy residents can be seen using cell phones all over the city.

Modern. Few people are as devoted to electronic gadgetry as are Hong Kong dwellers. A street vendor selling fresh fruit gazes at a portable color television between customers. People shopping in supermarkets chat on cellular phones as they push carts between the aisles. There are more cell phones per capita here than anywhere else in the world. City buildings are strikingly modern. In this ever-growing metropolis, buildings outlive their usefulness in just two decades. Twenty-story high-rises are routinely torn down to be replaced by forty-story structures. It seems the goal of the city's towers is to kiss the sky.

Modern Hong Kong is full of new skyscrapers (left) and, of course, the ever-present cell phones (below).

Noisy. Don't come to Hong Kong if you value peace and quiet. The streets are a symphony of noise. Air hammers rattle like machine guns on ever-present construction projects. Car radios blast so loud they sound like the rumblings of an earthquake. The radios are tuned to Chinese pop music or perhaps to Beethoven symphonies. But the notes are hardly distinguishable in the hurricane of sound. Cabdrivers are the biggest offenders. They play loud music constantly. Then they must turn their communication radios to the highest volume so they can hear their calls over the blast of musical programs.

Busy. Many men and women in Hong Kong escaped Communism just a few years ago. The escapees survived in Hong Kong on their wits and on their ability to work harder than the next person. No one forgets the rewards gained from hard work. From street sweepers to millionaire business owners, Hong Kong residents work at a pace that astonishes outsiders. Even schoolchildren hurry to classes as if they fear tardiness will somehow cause the world to end.

Chinese music blasting from car radios contributes to the high level of noise on the streets of Hong Kong.

Despite the residents' frantic work pace, Communism—the system they escaped from—has now enveloped their city. No matter. Job pressures continue. Duties must be performed. The big town buzzes with people frantically carrying on their work. A devotion to work is a Hong Kong trait that defies one-word descriptions. People work for money. Money has its own special place in Hong Kong life.

Everybody works in Hong Kong, including this woman watering flowers in Kowloon Park (left) and this vendor of name chops (seals) and calligraphy in the Stanley Market (above).

MONEY MADNESS

Notice the cars on Hong Kong's streets. Yes, some cars are little more than rolling wrecks. But look at the amazing number of luxury vehicles—BMWs, Mercedes-Benzes, Jaguars. Some of these cars cost more than an entire house in a tidy U.S. suburb. Look also at the modern town houses on the outskirts of the city. They are not huge. Many town houses contain only two or three bedrooms. Yet a well-placed town house costs from $30 million to $50 million. And there are people waiting in line to buy these pricey houses.

Some studies say there are more millionaires and billionaires in Hong Kong than in any other comparably sized city in the world. Many of these super-rich men and women were not born into their wealth. Some left Communist China carrying little more than the clothes on their backs. In capitalistic Hong Kong, they succeeded through energy, brains, and perhaps a touch of luck.

Certainly, Hong Kong holds legions of poor people. The poor and the middle class live in government housing projects that rise in layers like enormous wedding cakes. Some 60 percent of the city's population lives in government-subsidized housing. Housing projects are needed for poor people because land values here are the highest in the world.

A modern young Hong Kong couple at Wong Tai Sin Temple

In crowded Hong Kong, the old and the new, the
wealthy and the poor, exist side by side.
Above: The Sung Dynasty Village has a modern
condo high-rise as a background.
Right: Wash hangs outside a public housing building.

rickshaw (RIK-SHAW)

Rickshaws— A Symbol of Old Hong Kong

In the past, wealthy Europeans and Chinese got around the city by sitting in a rickshaw while a huffing and puffing puller tugged the vehicle through the streets. As late as the 1940s, there were 8,000 rickshaws registered in Hong Kong. Now, no licensed rickshaws remain. Nevertheless, scores of elderly rickshaw pullers stand with their vehicles along the harbor near the ferryboat terminals. Mostly they charge tourists a fee of $20 to $25 to sit in a rickshaw and pose for a snapshot. Sometimes they give people a ride, but beware of sky-high prices—as much as $150 for a five-minute pull.

By Asian standards, the poor of Hong Kong live well. Almost all hold jobs. The average income of Hong Kong's 6 million people is $23,000 a year. This is a higher average than that of Great Britain, the city's former master. By contrast, the average income in mainland China is only $650 annually.

Hong Kong factory workers enjoy air conditioning and indoor plumbing. They also have TVs and VCRs, items that only the well-off city people possess in China. And even the very poor of Hong Kong can at least dream about stepping up to the new ranks of the middle class.

Above: A man crosses a Hong Kong street on a bicycle.

Left: A Chinese farmer in the New Territories

Opposite page: Two schoolgirls use an umbrella to shield themselves from Hong Kong's hot sun.

Until the early 1980s, Hong Kong was divided into the haves and the have-nots. There was no in-between. Poor people worked to survive, not to climb the social ladder. But the Hong Kong economy now embraces a healthy middle class. The middle class includes doctors, bankers, and small businesspeople. Most of these newly middle-class people struggled to get an education and now insist that their children be well schooled. The existence of this middle class is a

Han Suyin (HAHN SOO-YIN
Tanka (DUNG-GAH)
Lu Tsun (LOW TSUNN)

The Boat People

Some Hong Kong residents live almost entirely on small boats that rest at anchor in the harbor. The most famous of these boat people is a small Chinese group called the Tanka. A folktale says the Tanka were once led by a general named Lu Tsun. Some two thousand years ago, Lu Tsun attempted to overthrow the emperor. The attempt failed, and as a punishment, Lu Tsun and his followers were forever banned from the Chinese mainland. In today's overcrowded city, the Tanka save rent by living aboard their tiny vessels. An estimated 35,000 Tanka reside on boats in Hong Kong Harbor.

reminder of the rewards gained by hard work—if such a reminder was ever needed among the industrious people of Hong Kong.

Why do Hong Kong people scramble so hard for money? Years ago, a Hong Kong novelist named Han Suyin pointed out that her city "works splendidly on borrowed time in a borrowed place." The novelist captured the key to the city's enormous energy. Fear drives the people to work and save their money. Hong Kong residents live in the shadow of a giant.

"I'll pray for Hong Kong, that it flies like a bird to the heavens, and you say a prayer for us."
—The departing words of Chris Patten, the last British governor of Hong Kong. Patten made this statement as he saw the Union Jack being lowered over the city for the final time.

THE FOUNDING

I n 1841, a British foreign minister described the site of Hong Kong as a "barren island with hardly a house upon it." That stark little island, which contained a few fishing villages, is today the modern city of Hong Kong.

Greed of the lowest form led to the city's founding. British people first moved to Hong Kong island in the 1840s to escape a violent upheaval called the Opium War. Opium is an addictive and dangerous drug that comes from the very beautiful poppy flower. In the early 1800s, British merchants based in the city of Canton earned fortunes smuggling the drug from India into China. As many as 2 million Chinese became hard-core opium addicts. The drug eroded Chinese society. The Chinese government demanded that the British stop selling opium to its people. The British refused, and the Opium War broke out in 1839.

The war was short and fought mainly at sea, where the British Navy had all the advantages. Heavy guns on British battleships blasted flimsy Chinese craft out of the water. China asked for peace and as a concession gave Hong Kong Island to the British. Hong Kong became a British colony in Asia. In its early years, the colony served as the headquarters for a massive drug trade that crippled the Chinese nation.

But sea captains also lauded Hong Kong for its splendid natural harbor. The words *Hong Kong* mean "Fragrant Harbor." Its deep, blue waters surrounded by a ring of mountains could provide safe refuge for whole fleets of ships. The splendid harbor made Hong Kong Island an ideal base from which to carry out the trade of legitimate goods.

A Chinese standard-bearer in the Opium War

Canton (KAN-TAHN)

The British attacking a Chinese junk during the Opium War

Because of the harbor, the territory expanded. In 1860, the British forced China to give them the Kowloon Peninsula, which lies across the harbor from Hong Kong Island. A city quickly grew on Kowloon. Thus, Hong Kong developed two major urban centers separated by a deep-water harbor.

In 1898, Britain leased a large region from China for a period of 99 years. The region covered 350 square miles (906 km^2) and included more than 230 islands. For lack of a better term, the leased area was called the New Territories. In 1997, when the lease ran out, it was still called the New Territories.

Left: The British assumed formal possession of Hong Kong in 1842.

THE LION VERSUS THE DRAGON

The lion has long been a symbol of British power while the dragon represents Chinese mystery. In Hong Kong, the lion and the dragon lived side by side. From the beginning, the two were stormy neighbors.

On a January morning in 1857, some 400 British colonists in Hong Kong sat over breakfast in their homes. As usual, the morning meal included tea and toast. Suddenly, scores of the colonists grew red-faced, gagged, and vomited. It was soon discovered that Chinese plotters had poisoned the bread dough at Hong Kong's favorite European bakery. The mass poisoning was a bold Chinese attempt to kill all the "foreign devils" at once. Miraculously, no colonists died. The identity of the plotters was never discovered.

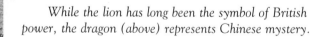

While the lion has long been the symbol of British power, the dragon (above) represents Chinese mystery.

Left: This illustration of Hong Kong and the harbor appeared in the Illustrated London News *in 1856.*

An 1883 view of Victoria Peak
as seen from the eastern hills

Hong Kong Colony was ruled by British officials who wore heavy white suits despite the sweltering sun. These British authorities insisted on enforcing their self-made decrees. The city had a European section and a Chinese section. The European section held theaters, fine hotels, banks, and grand government buildings. The much larger Chinese section was mostly a collection of shacks. Streets there were dark, dingy, and infested with drug-addicted criminals. A Chinese person who dared venture into the European district without permission could be arrested and beaten by police. Chinese were second-class citizens in a town that lay in the heart of Asia.

Despite such shabby treatment, Chinese people flocked to Hong Kong colony. Refugees came, often fleeing China in fear for their lives. A massive migration to Hong Kong began in 1911. That year, revolutionaries overthrew the long-standing Chinese government. The colony's population jumped to 500,000 by 1915. In 1937, Japan invaded China, and once more hordes of immigrants came to Hong Kong.

An illustration showing a southern Chinese farmer (left) and a businessman (right) in the 1880s.

Then, on the morning of December 8, 1941, the people of Hong Kong heard the scream of air-raid sirens. From over the sea came the rumble of plane engines. As terrified people fled the streets, the city shuddered under the thud of bombs. In a series of lightning attacks, Japan struck American bases and all European colonies in Asia. British, Canadian, and Hong Kong troops defending Hong Kong fought for two weeks but were outnumbered. On Christmas Day 1941, the colony surrendered to the Japanese army.

These American children were held by the Japanese in the Stanley Internment Camp in Hong Kong.

The occupying Japanese held about 400 Americans and 2,500 British citizens in the Stanley Internment Camp. These Americans posed for a picture shortly before they were taken to Africa for exchange with Japanese nationals.

For four years during World War II, the Japanese occupied Hong Kong. Japanese leaders used Hong Kong's magnificent harbor to supply its far-flung armies. Consequently, the city became a battleground as Allied bombers pounded shipping facilities. The population dropped by half as people fled the city. Also, the Japanese soldiers proved to be brutal occupiers. Hong Kong residents were required to bow in the presence of a Japanese army officer. Those failing to bow were kicked or clubbed by a soldier. The war and the terrible occupation brought Chinese and British Hong Kong people together as never before. The lion and the dragon had a common enemy in the Japanese. European and Chinese residents danced in the streets in September 1945 when the Japanese occupying army surrendered to British authorities.

On January 16, 1945, U.S. Navy planes attacked Hong Kong's Taikoo Dockyard. The Japanese did not surrender to British authorities until September 1945.

THE GIANT NEXT DOOR

After the war, turmoil in China continued to have an impact on Hong Kong. In 1949, the Communists declared victory in a civil war that had raged for years in China. The Communist triumph drove more than 1 million homeless and hungry refugees into Hong Kong. By 1950, an estimated 20,000 newcomers were entering the colony each week. The refugees were illegal immigrants, but British authorities did little to stop the human tide.

Many of the immigrants came from the Chinese city of Shanghai, a place long known for its aggressive businessmen. The former Shanghai residents set up tiny factories in Hong Kong basements. Those factories started a manufacturing revolution. At first, the tiny shops churned out plastic toys, flashlights, and small tools. Quickly, the shops shifted to making clothes and transistor radios. Hong Kong became, after Japan, the world's second-largest radio manufacturer. The bulk of these products were shipped to Europe and the United States. The words "Made in Hong Kong" became common on hundreds of items sold in the United States.

Bird toy

Shanghai (SHAHNG-HIGH)

A wide variety of goods, including toys like those shown here, are made in Hong Kong factories. Many artisans, however, work in narrow alley workshops. The man shown below is carving beautiful mythical birds to decorate a restaurant.

Dog toy

C. H. Tung became Hong Kong's chief executive on July 1, 1997.

C. H. Tung— From Refugee to Chief Executive

One of thousands of people who fled Communism in the late 1940s was twelve-year-old C. H. Tung. Like many other recent Hong Kong residents, Tung was from the city of Shanghai. His father was a prosperous ship owner. In Hong Kong, Tung entered the shipping business. True to the Shanghai tradition, he conducted business in a bold fashion and earned a fortune. In 1997, Tung was named by China to replace the British governor and lead Hong Kong as its chief executive.

The manufacturing revolution brought the prosperity that Hong Kong enjoys today. Manufacturing success was based on cheap labor, low taxes, and little government interference in business. An unwritten law held sway over government and business in the colony. The factories were owned by Chinese while the government was run by the British. As long as government gave business owners the freedom to operate their affairs, the Hong Kong money machine kept spinning. Hong Kong became a kingdom of capitalism on the shores of a Communist giant.

Still, the shadow of that giant loomed over the colony. In the late 1960s, the Cultural Revolution, a violent reaffirmation of Communism, swept mainland China. Young militants, called Red Guards, attacked and killed fellow citizens whom they believed were not proper Communists. The Cultural Revolution also triggered riots in Hong Kong. Then, in June of 1989, the world watched in horror as Chinese soldiers fought pro-democracy protestors near Tiananmen Square in the Chinese capital of Beijing. The Tiananmen Square battle reminded everyone that the Chinese Communist government dealt severely with people who dared question its authority. And those same Communist leaders would soon take over Hong Kong.

In 1984, Great Britain signed a treaty agreeing to transfer its colony to China on June 30, 1997. Technically, only the lease on the New Territories expired on that date. But since the New Territories comprise about 90 percent of the colony's total land area, all parties agreed that the transfer must include Hong Kong Island and Kowloon as well. What will be the future of Hong Kong under the Communist giant? Some Hong Kong people fear crackdowns like those that took place in Tiananmen Square. But many businesspeople believe life will go on more or less as it did under the British.

British ambassador Sir Richard Evans (seated, left) and Chinese assistant foreign minister Zhou Nan (seated, right) sign the 1984 agreement that paved the way for the 1997 transfer of Hong Kong from Great Britain to China.

The new leaders promise "one country, two systems." The Communists will run the government while the factory owners will continue to operate the economy. Businesspeople contend that China needs Hong

Tiananmen (TEE-ᴇɴɴ-AHN-MUNN)
Beijing (BAY-JING)

Left: The Chinese flag is raised at the ceremony marking the handover of Hong Kong to China just after midnight on July 1, 1997.

Below: Members of the Chinese armed forces honor guard stand at attention under the Chinese and British flags during the handover ceremony.

Kong's port and factory system to serve as a bridge between the Communist nation and the world. Why should Communist leaders kill a golden goose? Just before the takeover date, a reporter asked one Hong Kong factory owner what he thought would happen after June 30, 1997. The man shrugged his shoulders and said, "Probably July 1, 1997."

During Chinese New Year, the people of Hong Kong pay all their debts because they believe no one should start the coming year owing money. Factory workers are given bonuses and free dinners by their bosses. Children receive red envelopes containing "lucky money" from their parents. Strangers greet each other with the words, *Kung hay fat choi*, ("wishing you prosperity"). New Year is one of many holidays the festival-loving people of Hong Kong enjoy.

Kung hay fat choi
(GOONG HAY FAH CHOY)

CITY PEOPLE

What sort of people did China inherit in Hong Kong? About 98 percent of Hong Kong residents are Chinese. Other ethnic groups include Filipinos, Indians, Koreans, Japanese, Sephardic Jews from the Middle East, and British and American expatriates. The Chinese control the economy, owning 97 percent of the businesses. Most residents maintain traditional Chinese values, which include a healthy respect for their elders. Though hard work is accepted by all, a love of pleasure is built into the Hong Kong character. Few other people work harder or play harder than do Hong Kong citizens.

Hard work begins at an early age. Parents pressure children to study diligently even for kindergarten examinations. Acceptance at a prestigious kindergarten leads to acceptance at one of the better grammar schools, and a subsequent rise up the educational ladder. All Hong Kong children must attend classes until at least the age of fifteen. This drive for education has reaped rewards. In the 1920s, nine out of ten Hong

Above: Sisters standing in front of their home, which is decorated for the New Year celebration

Left: A Chinese student workbook

新雅

小學 中文 補充練習

附 模擬試題 及答案

小兔 盪秋千

Languages: Cantonese Versus Mandarin

Most classes in Hong Kong schoolrooms are taught in Cantonese, a language spoken in parts of southern China. Cantonese is spoken by 95 percent of Hong Kong people. But Mandarin, a very different language, is the official language of all China. At the changeover ceremony, Hong Kong's new chief executive, C. H. Tung, gave his acceptance speech in Mandarin. The speech caused many people in this politically sensitive city to fear that mainland leaders will one day compel them to speak Mandarin instead of their preferred Cantonese.

A Hong Kong schoolboy

Kong residents could not read or write. Today, nearly everyone is literate.

In Hong Kong, even pleasure is an industry. The city is one of Asia's greatest movie capitals. Hong Kong's studios churn out 50 films a year, giving it the nickname "Hollywood of the Far East." Films made in Hong Kong are popular in Chinese communities in Europe and in North America. Many Hong Kong-produced films are gory kick-boxing spectacles. And, like so much of Hong Kong life, films are more a business than an art form. When one studio owner was asked to name his best films, the owner said simply, "The ones that make money."

Cantonese (KAN-TUN-EEZ)
Mandarin (MAN-DUH-RINN)

Hong Kong tourists and residents alike love browsing in the city's many shops. Thousands of stores operate from complexes that look like the huge suburban shopping malls in North America. But many other goods are sold in open-air alleys crammed with tiny stalls. In these traditional markets, the flavor of old China survives in the modern city. Chinese herbal medicine stores sell exotic items such as powdered lizard, shark fins, and snake musk. Herbal medicine sellers claim these potions do everything from curing the common cold to easing the pain of rheumatism. At other stores, artisans stand behind benches painting tiles and pictures. Before the paint has dried, the artisans sell their creations to the spectators. Visitors to Hong Kong find an element of theater in the act of shopping.

Gambling is another Hong Kong pleasure, although many say it is the city's biggest vice. Devotion to horse racing is legendary. There are several newspapers dedicated entirely to racing news. Collectively, Hong Kong people bet U.S. $450 each year on

Chinese medicines are sold in bulk as well as in boxes and bottles such as these.

Above: The Shatin Racetrack
Left: A Chinese herbal medicine shop in the New Territories

Chinese herbs

horses for every man, woman, and child in the city. The new Shatin Racetrack is a technological marvel. A giant TV screen shows a slow-motion view of the horses galloping in at the finishing line. Shatin's computerized betting machines can process 1,500 bets per second.

The fast-paced game of mah-jongg also satisfies the people's penchant for gambling. Mah-jongg is similar to poker, but instead of cards the players use 144 small tiles that resemble dominoes. The sound of these tiles slapping on wooden tables becomes a roar outside the city's many mah-jongg parlors. By law, no money can be exchanged between the mah-jongg players. But judging by the excited cries and laughter coming out of the parlors, one can guess the people are not playing for toothpicks.

Shatin (SAH-TEEN)
mah-jongg (MAH-ZHONG)

LIFE AND LUCK

In 1988, a businessman paid the Hong Kong government $641,000 for a license plate on his car. The man was a million-aire many times over. But why should anyone buy a license plate worth even more than his automo-bile? The answer is sim-ple. The license plate bore the number 8, the businessman's lucky num-ber. Driving around with a number 8 plate would assure the man's contin-ued success in business.

Taoist good luck charms

Hong Kong residents are highly educated and comfortable with the gadgets of modern life. Operating a computer seems as natural to many of them as taking a walk. Yet they refuse to abandon old beliefs in the power of luck, fate, and supernatural forces.

Many Hong Kong men and women will not make a major decision without first consulting their favorite *feng shui* man. He is a combination priest, doctor, and financial consultant. A rich family moving to a new apartment will bring in a feng shui expert to determine how they should lay out the furniture. The furniture must be set down in a pattern so that spirits can move freely through the apartment. If the spirit bumps into a carelessly placed chair, it might become angry and do harm to the household.

Feng shui literally means "wind and water." This belief in the power of spiritual forces was brought to Hong Kong from China ages ago. Today, feng shui influences this sophisticated city in amazing ways.

In some cases, construction on a new downtown office building cannot begin until a feng shui master approves the building site. Is feng shui a silly superstition? No, say many Hong Kong people. Instead, it is a concept of balance—wind and water, spirit and life. Feng shui is as natural as the sunrise. Only fools would deny its power.

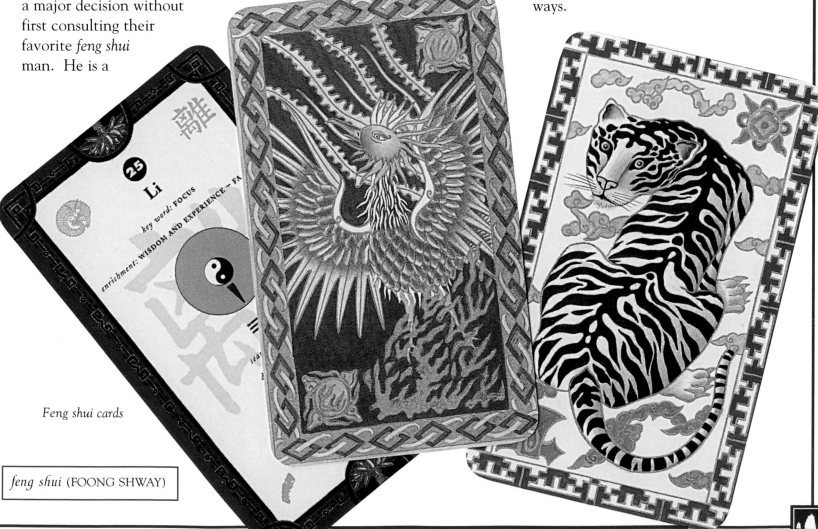

Feng shui cards

feng shui (FOONG SHWAY)

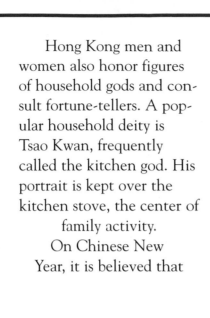

Hong Kong men and women also honor figures of household gods and consult fortune-tellers. A popular household deity is Tsao Kwan, frequently called the kitchen god. His portrait is kept over the kitchen stove, the center of family activity.

On Chinese New Year, it is believed that Tsao Kwan journeys to the heavens to tell his superiors which family members have been good or bad. Some children try to bribe Tsao Kwan by putting a dab of honey on his lips. Fortune-tellers are consulted by young people in love and by gamblers setting off to the mah-jongg parlors. Some fortune-tellers operate out of tiny booths. For a fee, they determine a customer's future either by reading palms or by shaking a cup full of small sticks and noting which sticks fall out.

Left: A statue of a Chinese goddess
Below: A Kowloon fortune-teller

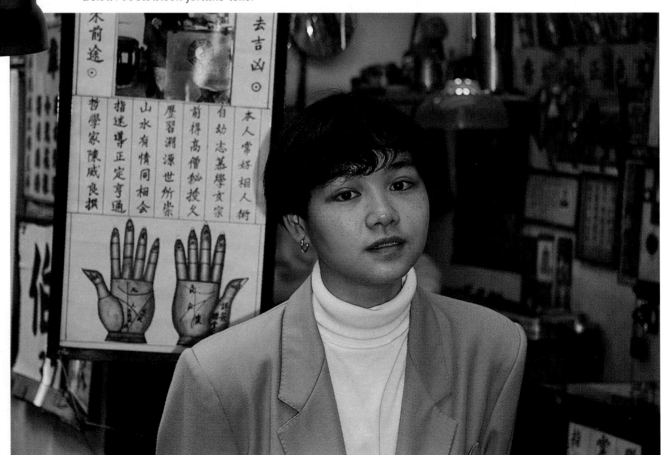

The Glory of Festivals

Hong Kong dwellers dot their calendars with a dozen different festivals. Many festivals are celebrated by the whole town. One is the Festival of the Hungry Ghosts. During festival time, families gather on the sidewalks where they burn papier-mâché figures of food, clothing, furniture, and money. It is believed that the spirits of dead relatives covet these items and will receive them as the figures go up in smoke.

THE PLEASURE OF FOOD

The huge floating restaurants in Aberdeen Harbor always attract crowds of diners.

Movie theaters in all cities advertise the names of the stars who appear in their current features. Hong Kong carries this star system to restaurants. In bold letters—or even in neon lights—restaurant owners display the names of their head cooks. Famous cooks have loyal fans and lure customers to the restaurant. The restaurant owner has to pay a small fortune to keep the services of a popular chef. If the chef accepts a job at a rival restaurant, thousands of customers will follow him there.

There are about 19,000 restaurants and cafes in Hong Kong. No other city of similar size has such a fantastic number of eating places. The reason for this abundance is simple. Hong Kong Chinese live to eat; they do not simply eat to live.

Restaurants vary from street-side stands where a bowl of noodle soup costs $4 to elegant dining rooms that charge more than $1,000 to feed a party of four. Poor people celebrate holidays by eating out rather than crowding a dozen or more people into their cramped apartments. For lunch, working men and women go to fast-food restaurants, including the

Stir-fried vegetables are a favorite Cantonese dish.

U.S. import, McDonald's. Because it is an international city, Hong Kong has restaurants that specialize in cuisines from around the world. Someone who enjoys variety will find French, German, Mexican, Italian, Indian, and Korean dining establishments.

Of course, Chinese restaurants prevail in this very Chinese city. But what is a Chinese restaurant? As Hong Kong residents will explain, Chinese food is regional. Meals vary remarkably from region to region in the huge land of China. Szechuan food, from western China, is known for its fiery spices. Cantonese food, from the region near the city of Canton, is noted for steamed vegetables and fish served with delicate sauces. Every region in China is deliciously represented in Hong Kong's wealth of restaurants. Visitors delight in sampling the marvelous cuisines of China all brought together in this one special city.

Chinese girls on a Hong Kong street

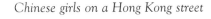
Szechuan (SECH-WAHN)

The great urban area that we know as Hong Kong is made up of three main centers—Hong Kong City, Kowloon, and the New Territories. Between Hong Kong Island and Kowloon is Hong Kong Harbor, which is about 1 mile (1.6 km) wide at its narrowest point. North on the Kowloon Peninsula are the mountains, islands, and farmland that are still called the New Territories. Hong Kong and its outlying regions contain marvels that a visitor will remember for a lifetime.

HONG KONG ISLAND

Hong Kong's city center sits on the north side of Hong Kong Island. Overlooking the harbor from Hong Kong is the Central District. This is the city's financial hub. Here stand the major banks, the stock exchange, and the imposing office buildings. One gleaming new structure is the Hong Kong Bank building, which cost $1 billion to complete. The Hong Kong Bank is said to be the costliest building in the world. Hong Kong people enjoy claiming they have the best of this or the biggest of that. For example, one city restaurant seats 7,000 diners and is said to be the biggest anywhere. Land in the Central District costs thousands of dollars per square foot. It is easily the most expensive land in the world.

Futuristic buildings dominate the Central District, but the neighborhood boasts many historic structures. Government House is a handsome white building erected in 1891. It used to be the official residence of the British governor. The city's oldest surviving building, built in 1846, is now the Museum of Tea Ware. Along with its collection of fine tea ware, the museum has an exhibit that explains the intricacies of brewing and serving tea.

Above: A ginger tea tin

The Man Mo Temple, built in 1847, is the oldest temple in Hong Kong.

The Man Mo Temple (1847) is the city's oldest temple. Its bell chimes regularly to attract the attention of the gods when prayers are being offered.

Hong Kong Island is also home to a neighborhood called the Western District, where many streets have a nineteenth-century look. It's fun to get lost in the Western District because there is a surprise around each corner. At the Western Market, artists paint mah-jongg tiles and sell them to shoppers. Fortune-tellers read palms with magnifying glasses. Other craftspeople carve jade or make colorful fans.

Man Mo (MUNN MOE)

Right: An artist painting fans
Below: A woman praying at the altar in Man Mo Temple

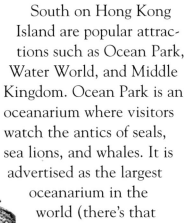

A view of the Middle Kingdom, a living museum that re-creates 5,000 years of Chinese history

This Chinese dancer is performing at the Middle Kingdom

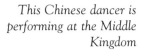

South on Hong Kong Island are popular attractions such as Ocean Park, Water World, and Middle Kingdom. Ocean Park is an oceanarium where visitors watch the antics of seals, sea lions, and whales. It is advertised as the largest oceanarium in the world (there's that boast again). Middle Kingdom is a living museum that re-creates 5,000 years of Chinese history. Kids love Water World, an aquatic fun park with water slides and pools that generate waves.

No visit to Hong Kong is complete without a trip to Victoria Peak, the 1,800-foot (549-meter)-high mountain that dominates the island. Tourists ride a cable-driven train called

The Dragon Boat Festival

A colorful Hong Kong festival is the race of the Dragon Boats, held in mid-June. A Dragon Boat is a long, slender canoe propelled by anywhere from twenty to fifty paddlers. The head of a dragon is often perched on its bow. According to legend, the race honors a Chinese poet named Chu Yuan. Some 2,000 years ago, Chu Yuan threw himself into the sea and drowned to protest government corruption. Now, so says the story, the Dragon Boats race to retrieve Chu Yuan's body. Spectators on shore set off firecrackers to cheer on their favorite vessel.

Chu Yuan (CHYOO YWAN)

the Peak Tram to reach the top. The Peak Tram opened for service in 1888, and is still used by thousands of people every day. Over the years, photographs taken from Victoria Peak show how Hong Kong has grown from a sleepy port to a dynamic city. Visitors on the Peak look down at the busy harbor and at their next destination—Kowloon.

Performers at the Middle Kingdom

KOWLOON

Kowloon lies directly across the harbor from the Central District of Hong Kong Island. To get there, people board the time-honored Star Ferry for an eight-minute boat ride. The deck of the Star Ferry offers an exciting view of the harbor. Commuters who are in a hurry zip over to Kowloon via an underwater subway. Separate automobile tunnels allow car traffic. Kowloon sits on the tip of the Kowloon Peninsula, which juts out of mainland China. It is a dense urban area where more than 2 million people live. The population of Kowloon is larger than that of Hong Kong Island.

A story says that centuries ago, a boy emperor hiked over the peninsula and found eight hills at the tip. The emperor called the place "eight dragons." Then a servant pointed out that the emperor was also considered to be a dragon. So the boy named it *gaulung* (nine dragons). The British later mispronounced *gaulung,* calling it "Kowloon." The name stuck. Today, the eight hills can hardly be seen. They have all been built over or excavated to create flat land for building sites. Much of the land scraped away from

This girl on the outskirts of Hong Kong is wearing traditional dress.

Kowloon was used to expand dock area at the harbor. Over the years, some 20 square miles (52 km²) of fill have been attached to Hong Kong's shores. This tendency to expand the shores is continuing. Some environmentalists fear the city's harbor will eventually shrink to the size of a river.

Kowloon is a curious mixture of tourist attractions and densely packed working-class neighborhoods. Along Nathan Road rise the city's most elegant hotels. Nearby are the Space Museum, the Hong Kong Museum of Art, and the Hong Kong Cultural Center. Also in Kowloon is a district called Mongkok. Here, workers and their families live packed together in rows of faceless housing projects. The only decorations on the project buildings come from the laundry that flutters on balconies.

Above: A child at a playground in Kowloon Park
Left: The Hong Kong Museum of Art

gaulung (GOW-LONG)
Mongkok (WONG-KAWK)

Two boat children in Aberdeen Harbor

Floating off the harbor in the Yaumatei District is a vast boat city. In the boat city, people can, if they choose, go for months without ever setting foot on solid ground. Residents shop at grocery boats and get their hair cut at barber boats. To reach their destinations, people simply hop from boat to boat in the crowded harbor.

Kowloon boasts some of Hong Kong's best-loved temples. The Tin Hau Temple has delicately curved roofs designed to ward off evil spirits. The Wong Tai Sin Temple is dedicated to a simple shepherd boy who lived years ago and had a magical gift for healing sick people. Sick people still come to the temple. The shepherd boy is known to be a generous spirit, eager to share his healing powers. Children love visiting the Temple of the Monkey God. He is a devilish spirit, a trouble-maker, a brat. The Monkey God was said to have been ousted from both heaven and hell because of his impish behavior. Still, he is a playful deity who amuses visitors. Even the strictest parents smile as they accompany children through the Monkey God's shrine.

A monk with an alms bowl at Wong Tai Sin Temple

Yaumatei (YOW-MAH-DAY)
Tin Hau (TEEN-HOW)
Wong Tai Sin (WONG DIE SIN)

A statue of the playful Monkey God

OUTLYING ATTRACTIONS

Hong Kong spreads out over 410 square miles (1,062 km²), including the New Territories and some 235 islands. People are concentrated in the urban areas because most of the outlying land consists of mountains and rocky islands scattered about the sea. Amazingly, a world of nature still exists right outside the crowded city.

On Sundays, city families escape their frantic neighborhoods for the peace offered by the country. Parks in the New Territories invite people to take hikes and nature walks. Here one sees traces of rural China's village life. In tiny ponds, farmers raise ducks intended for the city's restaurants. The Mai Po marshes in the New Territories are a popular gathering spot for bird-watchers. Tigers used to prowl the countryside here. The last wild leopard was spotted in the New Territories as late as 1957.

The Po Lin Monastery on Lantau Island

Hong Kong's largest island is Lantau. It is almost twice the size of Hong Kong Island. Windswept and rocky, Lantau used to be home only to a few fishing families and a group of Buddhist monks. Then, in the 1970s, developers discovered Lantau's splendid isolation.

Hotels and restaurants rose above its once lonely beaches. In the 1990s, the Chek Lap Kok Airport was built on the north side of Lantau. The airport is destined to be one of Asia's busiest.

Conservationists hope that Lantau Island is too rugged to support further large-scale development. Hong Kong residents need to visit uncrowded lands to take their minds off the pressures of urban life. Environmentalists have enjoyed some success in preserving the rural loveliness of Lamma Island. Lying south of Hong Kong Island, Lamma was once the home of fishing families. Living there now are people who have businesses in the city but prefer to live on the island. Lamma is sometimes called "Stone Age Island" because archaeologists have found remains of Stone Age people there. Nearby is Cheung Chau Island, which was once the lair of pirates. Many years ago, a mass grave of people probably killed by pirates was uncovered at Cheung Chau. A holy man recommended that the spirits of these victims be honored by a yearly festival. So, in late April, the islanders host a grand party that includes Chinese opera and fireworks.

Vessels of all descriptions weave between the islands to reach Hong Kong Harbor. That harbor has made Hong Kong one of the world's great cities. For generations, the British flag flew over the harbor's waters. Now the flag of China flutters there. So far, the people of Hong Kong have greeted this change with more hope than fear. Hong Kong residents know they live in a special city. It is a meeting place, a trading ground for many nations. Hong Kong's people hope that in the future, Hong Kong will be a vital bridge between China and the rest of the world.

A Cantonese opera star giving a performance in a Hong Kong theater

Mai Po (MY-POH)
Lamma (LAHM-AH)
Cheung Chau (CHEH-OONG TSOW)

FAMOUS LANDMARKS

The fountain inside the Landmark

Towers at the Central District's Exchange Square

Vegetable stalls at Stanley Market

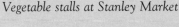

Vegetable stalls at Stanley Market

Government Office Building
Hong Kong's Government Office Building sits in the heart of the Central District. It is actually a complex that houses a concert hall, a theater, and several cultural affairs offices. It is also a place where young Hong Kong residents are issued marriage licenses. More than 6,500 marriages are performed there each year. Sentimental couples return on their anniversary to remember the magic moment.

Exchange Square
Much of Hong Kong society is dedicated to making money, and the Central District's Exchange Square is a symbol of that dedication. Exchange Square is a glass-and-steel complex of office towers that features the Hong Kong Stock Exchange building. Businesspeople claim that the stock exchange is the most modern in the world and tenants at Exchange Square insist they pay the highest rents on earth.

The Landmark
Certainly a landmark is a structure called the Landmark. Opened in 1980, the Landmark is an enclosed mall with more than 100 shops and a bubbling fountain in the middle. It is one of the more popular spots in the Central District.

Western Market
The Western Market lies in the heart of Hong Kong's Western District. In the modern city, this market is a throwback to an ancient Chinese gathering place. Here fortune-tellers and herb sellers abound. Artists paint customized mah-jongg tiles and chopsticks to suit customers' wishes.

Stanley Market
The name is very, very British, but the market is run entirely by Chinese merchants. It is made up of dozens of stalls whose owners specialize in selling clothes. Vendors boast that their dresses and suits are made from the finest material in the world, but they are priced low because of minor imperfections in the stitching. Years ago, the Stanley Market was hailed as a bargain-seeker's paradise. Today, veteran shoppers complain of its soaring prices.

A passenger boat and a houseboat in Aberdeen Harbor

The plaza and fountain, Kowloon Park

The Star Ferry

Aberdeen
Situated on the south side of Hong Kong Island, Aberdeen is a distant suburb of the city. It was once the lair of vicious pirates. Today, it still harbors the Tanka boat people, who live much of their lives on houseboats. Aberdeen is the jumping-off place for modern theme parks such as Ocean Park and Water World and the living museum called Middle Kingdom. Many tourists travel to Aberdeen to dine on board the famous floating restaurants.

The Star Ferry
Yes, there are now an underwater subway and three tunnels that link Hong Kong City with Kowloon. But everyone should take the Star Ferry boat at least once. The Hong Kong ferry has been operating since 1870. Today, its green-and-white double-decker boats make the trip every few minutes. Camera-toting tourists stand on deck snapping pictures of the skyline on both sides of this stunning harbor.

Kowloon Park
Kowloon is home to working-class tenement houses as well as luxury hotels where a room for a night costs more than a factory worker earns in a week. But rich and poor mix freely in Kowloon Park. It is a restful green oasis that features a lake and an aviary with a colorful collection of birds.

The Hong Kong History Museum
The story of Hong Kong is presented in this popular Kowloon museum. Life-sized dioramas show Hong Kong as a fishing village that existed long before history was written. Window by window, the dioramas progress to present the pain of the Japanese occupation and the triumph of modern Hong Kong.

FAST FACTS

POPULATION
The former colony as a whole: 6.3 million
Hong Kong City and Kowloon: 4 million

AREA
The former colony as a whole: 410 square miles (1,062 km²)
Urban areas: 23 square miles (60 km²)

LAND The urban area of Hong Kong is divided into three main centers—Hong Kong Island, Kowloon, and the New Territories. Hong Kong Island and Kowloon are separated by Hong Kong Harbor, a strip of water that is about 1 mile (1.6 km) wide at its narrowest point. Central Hong Kong is clustered along the harbor on the north side of Hong Kong Island. Urban Kowloon sits on the southern bank of the Kowloon Peninsula. The two urban centers are connected by an underwater subway, underwater car tunnels, and many ferryboats. The mainland portion of the Kowloon Peninsula, next to mainland China, is called the New Territories.

CLIMATE Hong Kong has a tropical climate. Summers can be torrid, with temperatures over 95 degrees Fahrenheit (35° Celsius) and high humidity. Winters are moderate and dry. Rarely does the January temperature fall below 50 degrees Fahrenheit (10° Celsius). It has never snowed in Hong Kong since records have been kept. Torrential rains can fall in the summer, causing floods.

INDUSTRIES The Hong Kong economy thrives on trade, banking, manufacturing, and tourism. About 80 percent of the people work in service industries such as banking. Hong Kong has more than 100 banks. It is the third most important financial city in the world, behind London and New York. Factories in Hong Kong produce electrical equipment, metal parts, and plastic goods. Many of the city's factory products are exported. The United States, Germany, Great Britain, and Japan are Hong Kong's biggest customers. In recent years, many factories have moved north into China where wages are lower. Hong Kong is a free port. No taxes are collected on the goods passing in and out of its harbor. Tax-free policies have made Hong Kong a world leader in finance and trade. Hong Kong Harbor is one of the world's busiest with 7,000 oceangoing cargo ships visiting it each year. Hong Kong's shops, restaurants, and elegant hotels delight tourists. Every year, more than 6 million tourists visit the city.

CHRONOLOGY

200 B.C.
Chinese settlements develop on Hong Kong Island.

Early 1600s
Europeans introduce the practice of opium smoking to China.

Late 1700s
Opium addiction becomes widespread in China; British merchants grow rich importing opium from India to China.

1800
China prohibits the importation of opium.

1839
The Opium War begins after Chinese government officials seize vast stocks of illegal opium from British merchants in Canton.

1841
British merchants raise the British flag over Hong Kong Island.

1842
The Treaty of Nanking officially ends the Opium War; China cedes Hong Kong Island to the British.

1857
Chinese plotters invade a British bakery and poison its bread; amazingly, no one dies.

1860
China cedes the Kowloon Peninsula to Great Britain; an urban area develops along the harbor.

1898
China leases the New Territories to Great Britain for 99 years.

1911
A violent revolution in China causes thousands of Chinese refugees to flee to Hong Kong.

Children carrying flags at the annual Cheung Chau Bun Festival

1931
Japan invades Manchuria (part of northern China), and more refugees enter Hong Kong colony.

1937
Japan invades Beijing and bombs Shanghai.

1941
Japan attacks Pearl Harbor and invades European colonies in the Pacific; the Japanese army occupies Hong Kong.

1945
Japan surrenders to the Allies; Hong Kong returns to British control.

1949
China becomes a Communist state after a long and bloody civil war; masses of Chinese escape to Hong Kong.

1966
The Cultural Revolution begins in China.

1967
Pro-Communists incite workers to riot on Hong Kong's streets.

1984
British and Chinese negotiators announce an agreement on Hong Kong's future status: Britain will hand over the entire colony to China in June 1997, when the lease on the New Territories expires; China promises to allow Hong Kong to keep its capitalist economy and way of life for fifty years after the takeover date.

1989
Chinese soldiers brutally put down a student demonstration at Tiananmen Square in the capital of Beijing.

1997
On June 30, British officials transfer Hong Kong to the Chinese government.

HONG KONG

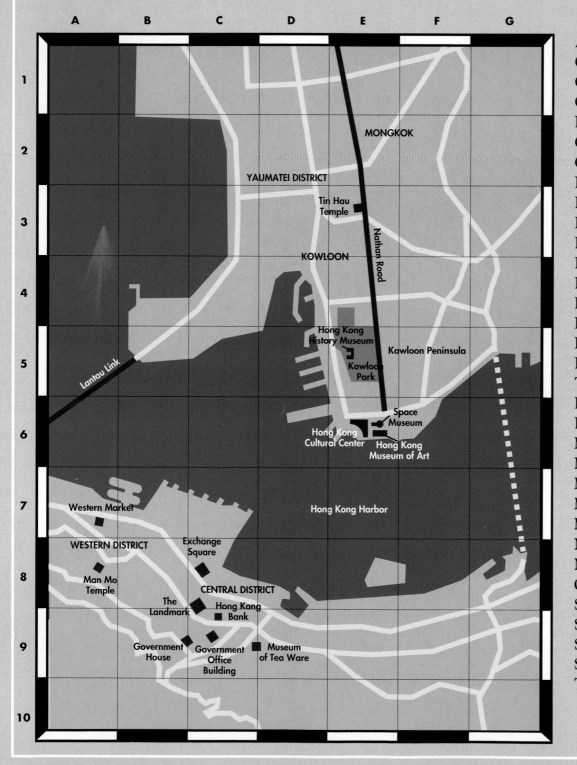

Aberdeen	J3
Central District	C,D 8
Chek Lap Kok Airport	H3
Cheung Chau Island	I4
Exchange Square	C8
Government House	B,C 9
Government Office Building	C9
Hong Kong Bank	C9
Hong Kong Cultural Center	E6
Hong Kong Harbor	A-G 5-8
Hong Kong History Museum	E5
Hong Kong Island	J,K 3,4
Hong Kong Museum of Art	E6
Kowloon	D,E 3,4
Kowloon Park	E5
Kowloon Peninsula	D-G 3-5
Lamma Island	J4
The Landmark	C 8,9
Lantau Island	H,I 3,4
Lantau Link	I,J 3
Mai Po Marshes	I1
Man Mo Temple	A8
Middle Kingdom	J4
Mongkok	E,F 2
Museum of Tea Ware	C,D 9
Nathan Road	E 1-6
New Territories	J2
Ocean Park	J4
Shatin Racetrack	K2
South China Sea	H-K 3,4
Space Museum	E6
Stanley Market	K4
Temple of the Monkey God	K3

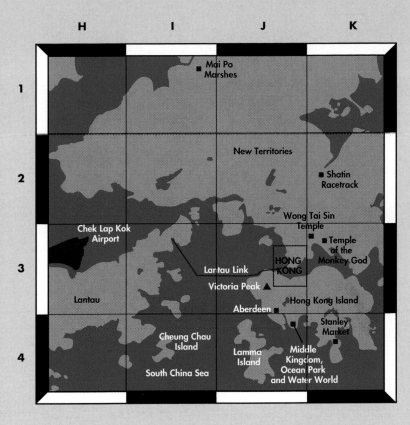

HONG KONG AND SURROUNDINGS

Tin Hau Temple	E3
Victoria Peak	J3
Water World	J4
Western District	A,B 8
Western Market	A7
Wong Tai Sin Temple	K3
Yaumatei District	C,D 2

GLOSSARY

cuisine: A style of preparing food, often associated with a nationality, such as Chinese, German, or Mexican cooking

decree: A law or an order issued by a government

deity: A god or spirit

expatriate: A person living in a foreign country

metropolis: A city

per capita: Per person or per head

plush: Very expensive, fancy

precedent-making: Having never occurred before

realm: A kingdom or an area of land

saga: A story or narrative

turmoil: Great confusion

upheaval: A violent event such as a war

vice: An evil or nasty habit

zest: Spirited enjoyment

Picture Identifications

Cover: A junk in Hong Kong Harbor and a child in Kowloon Park
Title Page: Children at a playground in Kowloon Park
Pages 4–5: A clerk selling T-shirts at a souvenir shop in Stanley Market
Pages 8–9: Boys in Hong Kong on bicycles
Pages 20–21: The illuminated skyline along Hong Kong Harbor was brightened with laser beams duiring the handover celebration on July 1, 1997
Page 21: Former Hong Kong governor Chris Patten (right) and Prince Charles boarding the *Britannia*
Pages 32–33: Tangerine trees, considered lucky by the Chinese, are colorfully decorated during the New Year season
Page 33: Chinese New Year "lucky money" in red envelopes
Pages 44–45: Hong Kong Island and Kowloon as seen from Victoria Peak at dusk

Photo Credits ©

SuperStock International, Inc. — Steve Vidler, cover (background), 48 (top), 49 (bottom); Bill Helms, 43 (top); Nigel Hicks, 55, 56 (right); Hidekazu Nishibata, 57 (middle)
Blaine Harrington III — Cover, (front left), 1, 6 (bottom), 15 (left), 51 (right)
KK&A, Ltd. — 3, 14, 24 (top), 28 (top left and bottom right), 33, 34 (bottom), 36 (left), 39, 40 (top), 46 (top), 53 (right), 60, 61
Robert Fried — 4–5, 6 (top), 15 (right), 16; Sophie Dauwe, 19 (right)
Photri, Inc. — 7, 36–37, 47 (right), 56 (left); Prenzel, 54
Unicorn Stock Photos — Jeff Greenberg/MRP, 8–9
Tony Stone Images, Inc. — Keith MacGregor, 10; Sylvain Grandadam, 11 (bottom), 57 (left); Paul Harris, 18 (right), 38; John Lawrence, 44–45; Rex A. Butcher, 47 (left)
Impact Visuals — Donna De Cesare, 11 (top); Sean Sprague, 13 (right)
Cameramann International, Ltd. — 12 (left), 13 (left), 19 (left), 34 (top), 35 (bottom), 37 (right), 42, 52, 56 (middle), 57 (right)
New England Stock Photos — Jean Higgins, 12 (right); Russell Gordon, 41
Comstock — 59; Franklin J. Viola, 17 (left)
Carl Purcell — 17 (right), 35 (top), 40 (bottom)
Root Resources — Byron Crader, 18 (left)
AP/Wide World Photos — 20–21, 26 (both pictures), 28 (bottom left), 30–31, 31 (bottom right)
Agence France Presse/Corbis-Bettmann — 21
North Wind Picture Archives — 22, 25 (bottom)
Stock Montage, Inc. — 23 (top)
Corbis-Bettmann — 23 (bottom)
Mary Evans Picture Library — 24 (bottom), 25 (top)
UPI/Corbis-Bettmann — 27, 30 (bottom left)
Archive Photos — Reuters/South China Morning Post, 29
Dave G. Houser — 32–33, 43 (bottom); Jan Butchofsky-Houser, 46 (bottom), 50–51, 53 (left); John Gottberg, 49 (top)
Travel Stock — Buddy Mays, 48 (bottom), 50 (left)

INDEX

Page numbers in boldface type indicate illustrations

Aberdeen, **42, 52,** 57, **57**
air travel, 10–11, 55
automobiles, 16
Americans, **26,** 34

Beijing, 30, 59
boat people, 19, **52,** 53, 57

Canton, 22, 43, 58
Cantonese, 35, 43
capitalism, 6, 16, 29, 59
cell phones, **12,** 13, **13**
Central District, 46, 50, 56
Chek Lap Kok Airport, 10–11, 55
Cheung Chau Bun Festival, **59**
Cheung Chau Island, 55
China, 5, 10
    Communism in, 6, 14, 15, 16, 28, 30–31, 59
    income level in, 18
    Japanese invasion of, 25, 59
    transfer of Hong Kong to, **4–5,** 5, **6–7, 6, 7, 20–21,** 21, 30–31, **31,** 59
Chinese New Year, **32–33,** 33, **34,** 40
Chinese settlements, 25, 58
Chu Yuan, 49
climate, **18,** 25, 58
Communism, 6, 14, 15, 16, 28, 30–31, 59
crafts, **28,** 47, **47**
Cultural Revolution, 30, 59

economy, 6, 18, 29, 34, 58
education, 14, 18, 34, **34,** 35, **35**
ethnic people, 19, 34
Exchange Square, 56, **56**

farming, **18, 25,** 45, 54
feng shui, 39, **39**
festivals, **32–33,** 33, **34,** 41, **41,** 49, **49,** 55, 59
foods, 9, 42–43, **43**
fortune-tellers, 40, **40**

gambling, 36–37, **37**
Government House, 46
Government Office Building, 56
Great Britain, 5, 18, 22, 46
    expiration of lease over New Territories, 30, 59
    possession of Hong Kong by, 23–27, **23,** 58
    transfer of Hong Kong, to Chinese, **4–5,** 5, **6–7, 6, 7, 20–21,** 21, 30–31, **31,** 59

Han Suyin, 19
herbal medicine, 36, **36, 37,** 56
history, 22–31, 58–59
Hong Kong Bank building, 46
Hong Kong City, 45, 57
Hong Kong Cultural Center, 51
Hong Kong Harbor, **cover,** 6, 10, **10,** 19, **20–21,** 22, 23, **24,** 27, 45, 50, 51, 55, 57, 58
Hong Kong Island, 10, 30, **44–45,** 45, 46–49, **46, 47, 48, 49,** 50, 55, 57, 58
housing, 12, 16, **16,** 42, 51, 57

income level, 18
industries, 58

Japan
    invasion of China by, 25, 59
    and World War II, 26–27, **26, 27,** 59

Kowloon, 10, 23, 30, **44–45,** 45, 49, 50–53, **50, 51,** 57, 58
Kowloon Park, **cover, 1,** 15, **51,** 57, **57**

Lamma Island, 55
Landmark, the, 56, **56**
languages, 35
Lantau Island, **54,** 55
Lantau Link, 11
literacy, 35

mah-jongg, 37, 40, 47, 56
Mai Po marshes, 54
Manchuria, 59
Mandarin, 35
manufacturing revolution, 28–29
Middle Kingdom, 48, **48, 49,** 57
Mongkok, 51
Monkey God, 53, **53**
movies, 35
museums, 46, 48, **48,** 51, **51,** 57
music, 14, **14**

New Territories, 23, 45, 54, 58
    expiration of British lease of, 30, 59
    lease of, 23, 58

Ocean Park, 48, 57
opium, 22, 58
Opium War, **22,** 22, **23,** 58

Peak Tram, 48–49
Pearl Harbor, 59
Po Lin Monastery, **54**
population, 10, 12, 18, 25, 27, 50, 58

refugees, 25, 28, 58, 59
restaurants, 42, **42,** 46, 54, 57, 58

Shanghai, 28, 29, 59
Shatin Racetrack, 37, **37**
shopping, 13, 36, **36,** 47, 56, 58
skyscrapers, 10, 13, **13, 17**
South China Sea, 11
Stanley Internment Camp, **26**
Stanley Market, **4–5, 15,** 56, **56**
Star Ferry, 50, 57, **57**
Stone Age Island, 55
subways, **11,** 50, 57, 58
Sung Dynasty Village, **17**
superstitions, 38–40, **38, 39, 40**
Szechuan, 43

Taikoo Dockyard, **27**
Taoist good luck charms, 38, **38**
temples, **46,** 47, **47,** 53, **53**
Tiananmen Square, 30, 59
tourism, 9, 10, 11, **11,** 12, 17, 36, 48–49, 51, 57, 58
trade, 22, 28, **28,** 55, 58
transportation, **8–9,** 10–11, 16, 17, **18,** 50, 57, 58
Treaty of Nanking, 58
Tung, C. H., 29, **29,** 35

Victoria Peak, **10, 25, 44–45,** 48–49

Water World, 48, 57
Western District, 47, 56
Western Market, 56
work ethic, 9, 14, 15, 18, 19, 34
World War II, 26–27, **26, 27,** 59

Yaumatei District, 53

TO FIND OUT MORE

BOOKS

Fodor's Hong Kong 1998: The Complete Guide with Walking Tours and Excursions to China and Macau. New York: Fodor's Travel Publications, Inc., 1997.

Fyson, Nance Lui. *Hong Kong.* World in View series. Austin, Texas: Steck–Vaughn Library, 1991.

Grzeskowiak, Andrew. *Passport Hong Kong: Your Pocket Guide to Hong Kong Business, Customs, and Etiquette.* San Rafael, Calif.: World Trade Press, 1996.

Halvorsen, Francine. *The Food and Cooking of China: An Exploration of Chinese Cuisine in the Provinces and Cities of China, Hong Kong, and Taiwan.* New York: John Wiley & Sons, 1996.

Huang, Evelyn and Lawrence Jeffrey. *Hong Kong: Portraits of Power.* London: Weidenfeld & Nicolson, 1995.

Jacobsen, Peter Otto and Preben Sejer Kristensen. *A Family in Hong Kong.* Families Around the World series. New York: Bookwright Press, 1985.

Krannish, Ronald L. *The Treasures and Pleasures of Hong Kong.* Impact Guide series. Manassas Park, Virginia: Impact Publications, 1996.

Wue, Roberta. *Picturing Hong Kong: Photography 1855–1910.* New York: George Braziller, Inc., 1997.

ONLINE SITES

Hong Kong Mensa
http://home.hkstar.com/~hkmensa/
Learn about this worldwide organization for people with high IQs. Take a sample IQ test, solve puzzles, and more. Good luck!

Hong Kong Science Museum
http://www.usd.gov.hk/CE/Museum/Science/index.htm
Tour the museum to see changing exhibits, and learn about a variety of topics and upcoming events.

Hong Kong Observatory
http://www.info.gov.hk/hko/contente.htm
No stars and planets, but plenty about earthquakes, cyclones, and other weather conditions as they relate to Hong Kong.

Hong Kong Wonder Net
http://www.hkta.org/
Current events, festivals, sightseeing, clickable maps, photos, lots of links.

Mandarin Films
http://www.mandarin.films.com/hk/
Visit the virtual theater, where you can check out the company's films currently playing in Hong Kong. Get story descriptions and photos from the movies. You can even watch film clips (if you have the software and the time).

Radio and Television
http://www.rthk.org.hk/
See clips from actual television shows, listen to radio programs, and get 24-hour news from Hong Kong!

South China Morning Post
http://www.scmp.com/
Browse "Hong Kong's Leading English-Language Newspaper Since 1903."

University of Hong Kong
http://www.hku.hk/
Glimpse university life at one of Hong Kong's leading educational institutions—history and background, departments, statistics, and upcoming events.

ABOUT THE AUTHOR

R. Conrad Stein was born in Chicago. After serving in the Marine Corps, he attended the University of Illinois where he received a degree in history. Mr. Stein is a full-time writer of material for young readers. He has published more than 80 books. The author lives in Chicago with his wife and their daughter, Janna.